Amazement

Ramona S. Bostic

AMAZEMENT
Copyright © 2020 by Ramona S. Bostic

All rights reserved. No part of this publication may be reproduced, distributed, or transmitted in any form or by any means, including photocopying, recording, or other electronic or mechanical methods, without the prior written permission of the publisher or author, except in the case of brief quotations embodied in critical reviews and certain other noncommercial uses permitted by copyright law.

Although every precaution has been taken to verify the accuracy of the information contained herein, the author and publisher assume no responsibility for any errors or omissions. No liability is assumed for damages that may result from the use of information contained within.

Library of Congress Control Number: 2018954677
ISBN-13: Paperback: 978-1-64398-204-5
PDF: 978-1-64398-205-2
ePub: 978-1-64398-206-9
Kindle: 978-1-64398-207-6
Hardcover: 978-1-64398-208-3

Printed in the United States of America

LitFire LLC
1-800-511-9787
www.litfirepublishing.com
order@litfirepublishing.com

Contents

INTRODUCTION V
DEDICATION VII
    Beyond Looks 1
    Moms Are Love! 2
    VALENTINE... 3
    MOM 4
    MOTHER'S DAY 5
    HAPPY FATHER'S DAY 6
    CAREGIVERS 7
    HARK 8
    That Hometown Prince 9
NATURE'S JOY 13
    Love Denied 15
    What A Hug! 16
    In My Dream 17
    A Heroes Salute! 18
    God's Gift 19
    Halo 20
    Do I Miss You? 21
    Friends 22
    A Sparrows Song 24
    Father's Day 25
    Glorious Love 26
    The Unique One! 27
A DOVE'S TALE 29
UNCLE ED 31
    A Pest? 33

Cest La Vie-That's Life!	34
Is A Bird Free?	35
PEACE AT LAST	**37**
In Memoriam	39
Sprung!	40
The Signs	41
Limerick 1—Hillary	42
Limerick 2—Obama	43
Molasses	44

Introduction

*P*oetry and short-fiction are, Miss Bostic's forte. She is her own kind of writer. Loving creatures of Nature as subjects, and rhyme in her poetry. Ramona shares little with Shakespeare, some with Longfello yet she shares hardly as much as she would like with our "Beloved, Maya AngeLou." Ramona's main focus in her literature, is the youth and young at heart! Her, "Spring Has Sprung!", "Halo" and "Pest?" are a few of the poems; not to mention, her short-fiction, that attest to this! Why don't you, her many readers, from then and now Enter-In & Read On!

Dedication

God, our Heavenly Father-First and Foremost! The Pastors, Dads, Father-figures and close-friends, who are always there to pick-up the pieces or put a smile where a frown once was. We, the dedicators are indebted to you, because; You were there when we needed you. And always you came to our side when we called or a tear we cried. It was you, who made us see the light when our life seemed dark and full of fright. We can say many more words, we believe you know. The fact is; we love you and it grows! Happy Fathers Day Glory Be to the Father and to The Son and To The Holy Ghost.

Beyond Looks

Ravaged with acne all over her face
Her hirsute legs are hidden with lace

A new double-chin and a gray-hair or two
A deep-down-gut feeling she would rather be you

Yes, Something in-side her,
Sees oh, so much further

She is thankful to God
for her Father and Mother

Think what a bitter pill she has not to swallow
Because she can dream a brighter tomorrow

When it's all over and the mirror has broken

She will have known all along, that
Looks are merely a Token!

Circa 1951 "The Bostics"

Moms Are Love!

Sons

*I Love you from the Inside Out
Let there Never be A Doubt!
You have always been my Mom-indeed!*

*If left to me, there would be More days
To Honor you in Varied ways
May your Mother's Day be as Special to you
As your L-O-V-E has been more than Special to ME!
I Love you Mom!*

VALENTINE...

U-R-So Cool!
U-R-So Fine!

Won't You
Be-Mine?

Roses are red
Violets are Blue
I have decided
That
My Valentine has
To Be Y-O-U!

MOM

You — R —The
GREATEST!
You are loved
By the flowers
You are Loved
By the trees
You are Loved
By the birds
You are Loved
By the bees!
Most of all…
You are Loved, by
Yours Tru — ly!
HAPPY MOTHER'S DAY!

MOTHER'S DAY

*Do you
Know
U — R — Special?*

*Mom, it took
The strength and
Love of a gal like you,*

*To tame the likes
Of a tuff little
Tyke like me-then!*

Have a Wonderful Mother's Day!

HAPPY FATHER'S DAY

Sons

Good Dads have
A place in the hearts of us all
And you have had that space,
since you were small
Be kind to your Toddlers
Be true to your wife
No doubts, my son
You will have a great life!

Happy Father's Day!

CAREGIVERS

Fathers and Caregivers
Are Special too!
Like Mothers,
"They" comfort and offer
Tenderness, in all that they do!

To each and every one of you
Here is some Love
And warm wishes Too!

HARK

The Herald Angels Sing.
This day is Special,
I'd like to say, 'cause Christ,
our Lord was born today!

Whether, Santa comes down the
The chimney, or not,
It is Christ, we
Ought thank, for All we got!

Merry Christmas, to all
And
To all, a Good Night.

That Hometown Prince

*I was so slow
He was so lean
I, his tortoise"
He, my "stringbean."*

*He hailed from the East
I from the West
He, ever so keen
I was next on his list!*

*We laughed-And –
We cried
Love soared-Then –
Love died!*

*Never, will I forget my
Prince from the East
This man I adored
Soon seemed like a beast*

Like sand of the desert
From whence he had come
Feigned love dissipated
Now, what had he done?

Thus, I have learned
To remain here at home
To never again
Let my heart out to roam!

All you young ladies
Attracted to men
From other oases
Think it over again

You ought heed my warning
Beware of the lies
From your Super Hero
In his "Clark Kent" disguise.

Learn all about him
His plans, his beliefs

Take care, he's not
Just another heart thief

Enjoy your quaint sweetheart,
Your caballero, your king
But sure as time passes
And you haven't that ring

Remember One Thing:

It may behoove you to notice
The young man next door
Don't feel disgruntled, upset,
Don't even dread

Many-a-princess
Were crowned
Whence that hometown prince
They did wed!

Nature's Joy

One day I was helping Mom wrap an old, tattered shawl over her shoulders. Mom was getting up-in age then, yet by nature was frail and always cold. As the Autumn/Winter Seasons were quickly approaching; here in New England, we were aware of the annoying chills. Life had become quite, ho-hum, in our small town of Peaceville Massachusetts. With little excitement, to speak-of, Mom and I were all each other had.

In Mom's room, which was sparsely furnished, yet had plenty of open space; I was transfixed by an odd-romping about on Mom's, carpeted, bed-room floor. I nudged Mom and said, "Will you look at that!" There on her bedroom, floor scampering-about, were what looked-like: two rodents; one, large with a long, furry tail; the other, small with a short furry tail. There was no mistaken these, dear, creatures of nature, were indeed, squirrels! The Larger squirrel, I take it, the mother, was chasing the minor and nipping on its rear-end. As she did so, she turned around for a hasty moment; peered into my face with trusting eyes. She then chirped, 'That is my son and he is adventuresome just like his father. You see, I'm attempting to curb his energy, so he can grow-up gradually. He has so much to learn about life.

You understand?" she queried. I nodded my head positive. The squirrels' romping-about abruptly, came to a halt. Of all things, they raised-up on their grayish-brown, haunches and assumed a begging stance. You got it, Common Beggars, they were. I recognized this pose, 'cause years ago, I would walk through a local, famous park and cater to the squirrels, there. Their little "act" is unique and irresistible. Mom fell for this act long before I. She introduced me, as she was an avid furry-creature lover from "git."

I fled to the kitchen, cabinet where we kept a bag of roasted peanuts. I was first to scoop up a handful of the fresh-smelling p'nuts. Next, I bent down to the level of the two gray, furry beggars and doled the roasted, p'nuts out, one-by-one. These hungry critters clutched each peanut betwixt their human-hand-like paws. These nuts were still encased in the original shells. The squirrels nibbled away until the peanuts were no more! Mom participated, rather, gleefully too. I saw it in her, twinkly, blue eyes. This brought joy to my heart!

As quickly, as these fascinating, little, rodents had appeared; as quickly did they disappear. However, the miniature epic with these trusting creatures of Nature, provided Mom and me with an experience of undeniable Joy!

Love Denied

I now, know I loved you
Just as you loved me
However, you knew that we were close
And I did Not
Your day came and
Never had I said
That you were Special too.
Although you did tell your friends of me
I refrained from telling mine of you.
My heart is heavy, because I really Miss you
My soul is empty
If you were with me now,
I know you would forgive me
Yet, can I ever Forgive Myself?
No, I cannot!
Thus, I can say
"I am proud of you, Mom
Because, you never let me know
That I caused you pain;
And you protected me,
I was always, your Darling Daughter'
And you, were and Always will be
My 'Beloved Mother!"

What A Hug!

What a wonderful hug
That I got yesterday
It is a hug that will stay with me
For many-a-decade
It came from a man that I admire
In many-a-way

This hug had no strange nor
Peculiar power
Instead, it was very comforting
In that Special hour.

In My Dream

I dreamed — a dream, a dream of you
It brought me near again to you
The dream: It said: so many things
It told of Love, of Loss, of Pain.
I miss you deeply, that is a Fact!
So in my dream, I bring you back!

A Heroes Salute!

Thank God for our Military
And Veterans, one and All!
Are you not overwhelmed, that they accepted their call?

These Men and Women are many
And we best believe;
They are all Heroes too!
How many deferred their hopes and ambitions
for our Red, White and Blue?
Our world is indebted. Do we all agree?
These Military personnel and Veterans
Are the reasons why,
We can declare ourselves "Free."
Give Them your Blessings and pause ... to
Honor every person who has served this country in A Branch
of the Military...every day you wake up and you realize
"Freedom Is Not free!"

God's Gift

I saw a pretty butterfly
fluttering about the earth.
As it pursued the Heavens above
Mother Nature said, "Defer."

Flowers yield their, nectar,
Menacing in the shadows,
Looms man with his net!
Reason why this Gift from God
Has the instinct to flit and flit.

This marvelous, winged/insect,
is inherently, elusive,
And gently, peaceful 'too.
Never to be-friend man.
Why? Innately, that is taboo!

The presence of this Gift from God
Is a wonder to behold!
It doesn't matter, who you are.
You are neither-too young nor
Too old!

Halo

Halo, halo
What are you doin' there?
Just above my head
and messin' up my hair?
I told you, I am a sinner
But it seems,
you just don't care!
Now, when The Chief comes down
to greet me, from way-up in the air;
I will say, "Blame your naughty, halo, Lord,
'cause I don't have a Prayer!"

Do I Miss You?

Do I Miss You Moms? You bet I do!
Do I Miss you dad? Of course I do!
My only Bro, alas, the last to go!
Where did they go? I do not Know!
Oh, it Makes me wander, and I pace to and fro!
Yes, I believe in God above, and feel the comfort of His Love
'Cause when His call shall come to me;
It's with my long, lost kin again I'll be.

Friends

What is it about This world
That exists

Where is our Love, our Compassion
Our Fellowship

Did they Desist?

The flowers the trees, the birds and the Bees
The Moon the stars, Venus and Mars

All Co-exist!

Yet, we as humans-one another-Resist!

We have in common, oh, so many things

But, some say, Is it the COLOR of our skin
That means Every Thing?!

The splendor of the myriad flowers abloom
Mesmerize us, their variety so unassumed.

The call to Arms brings us together for
Peace sake

When war is over, worse is the inherent Hate!

I do you-you do me is this Not sin?
How could we, Why do we,
When did such ignorance Begin?

Well, I say, It's time for this foolishness
To End!

Begin to Love! Let go of Hate! Embrace and
Let's be Friends.

A Sparrows Song

Have You ever heard a sparrow's song?
It has a melody that is vibrant and clear
A sparrow's song brings a tingly delight
to each and every ear
When ever I hear the Sparrow song,
I stop what ever I do
Because, it is what I need
To thrill me through and through!
As a sparrow trills through-out the air
This causes me to think,
God gave this song
To this lilting, little "Thing!"
A sparrow's song gives joy to all
You can hear most every day
Now, when You hear the sparrow's song
'Twill take your breath away.

Father's Day

(a note)

I am indebted to you cause,
You were there when I needed you!

Dear Pa: You were always on the line
when I called and cried a tear...
You and "Ma" showed me light; as, usually
My life was dark and mostly full of fear!

I can go on with more prose, I believe
You know,
Guess one thing, I love you ... and it grows!

Happy Father's Day!

Glorious Love

Cheerful as a sparrow's song
Is how I feel, today
'Cause God has blessed me with His love
In many-a-splendid way
The sun, the moon, the stars above
Are proof that He is real
Yet, though this is a testament,
It is for from any spiel
Oh, how His spirit fills my soul as my life, flows along.
It seeps inside my heart, that tolls, with mirth, and joy and song!

My world is truly, more complete, and I shall not complain.
Because God's unconditional love, surpasses all refrains!

The Unique One!

A Dog or a Cat-your choice for a pet?
You think your choice is the Best one yet?
A furry creature to have and to hold?
Could a dog or a cat be easier to mold?
Have you never thought to try to care
For another furry creature, maybe even a bear?
I'd try a purple rabbit but only in my dream.
Not a reality, yet really supreme!
Unusual creatures can also be true.
Do consider a squirrel, a possum or even a kangaroo.
A Dog or Cat is hardly my choice!
They're for too common, with a lackluster voice!
I'll take a chimpanzee, a koala, or Maybe a mole.
And, 'cause each is unique, it should be food for my soul.
Give me the unusual, demonstrative ones, 'cause in my mind;
They are Intriguing, and More fun!

A Dove's Tale

*L*et me pick two beautiful winged creatures; in particular, butterflies and bumblebees. These two are at the opposite end of the spectrum. Being quite the dove that I am, I was flying subtlely above a Monarch butterfly and a bumblebee. They were discussing Man as he exists now and yesterday. Since the days of my ancestors, man' has remained the same (abominable). My ancestors go back to the days of Noah and his Ark; it was an ancestor of mine who brought the twig to Noah.

Dig what I overheard in flight: "You know, Bubba Bee, if humankind ever noticed us in the air together, they'd flip {chuckle}," "You know what else, Beautyfly, we are the least they'd expect to see together; I only sting them because they are the wretched of the earth." "Humankind hates one another for no particular reason and make laws and rules only to break them: the 10 Commandments and the Golden Rule are prime examples." "Also, Bubba Bee, humans don't realize how much that they ought to be thankful for."

"Humans live a long life whereas insects live from season to season. Besides gathering honey for ourselves we are slaves to man. They want our honey and our honey combs." "Well, Bubba, God has been good to us; we do everything by *instinct which is natural so we need not feel guilty about what goes on in the course of our short lives."*

"You know, Bubba, I never told you why I flit so fast; it's so humans can't catch me with those awful nets that they think will get them specimens to examine. Then when they're thru with their dirty work, we wind up in the trash-dead too."

"Bubba, What kind of Creatures are these?" "Never mind, Beauty; that's exactly why Mother Nature instilled all innocent creatures with the fear of man. Man knows not of love."

Being a dove is not fear-free either; man has plenty of stupid uses for us too; such as being a pet in a cage or being stuffed in some magician's hat. Doves are still peaceful creatures. As a wise ol' owl once told me: "There is still hope for man; only because God is a forgiving God."

Uncle Ed

*U*ncle Ed and his family hailed from the state of Missouri. Ed and his wife had two teenage daughters and a five-year-old son. Their blessings were many and their problems were few, with one exception. Their magnificent hacienda was infiltrated with a common enemy of most any household—a rodent extraordinaire—a rat! And no, his name was not "Mickey"! Try as he may, Uncle Ed could not rid his house of this pet-I mean pest! One balmy afternoon while leafing through one of his many sports magazines, an interesting story caught the intent eye of Uncle Ed. The story was that of a frustrated fisherman. At one time, the top in his sport, this fisherman was experiencing hard times, especially since this was the means of his livelihood.

One day a bit of an absurd idea came to this "catcher-of-fish." He placed a photo of a succulent worm at the end of his hook and cast his line in the water. He waited patiently for what he thought would be "a pleasant surprise," a "prize catch!" Without reading another word, Ed leapt out of his recliner and embarked on a search. Uncle Ed was in search of a photo of an enticing piece of cheese, holes and all! This Ed found in his wife's "Good Housekeeping" magazine. The photo was inserted with the utmost of care in his very expensive not-so-effective rat trap. This was done not without saying, "with Great Expectations!"

Having done that, Uncle Ed decided to finish reading about his sports counterpart-the fisherman. You guessed it-the fisherman was up against a cruel twist of fate. At the first tug on his line, the fisherman reeled his line in. No longer was the picture of a worm on his hook, but in its place was a picture of a fish.

That night, while tossing and turning in his bed with much anticipation, Ed felt that his plan would hardly be that of the frustrated fisherman. At about midnight, Uncle Ed heard without a doubt what must be the rat trap-"Got him" he thought finally!" Upon jumping out of bed and turning on the kitchen light where the trap had been placed, Ed's eyes focused on the trap. There in the trap was no longer a photo of the enticing piece of cheese with holes and all, but-you guessed again—in its place was the photo of rodent extraordinaire—a rat, grinning from ear to ear.

Remember an old adage adapted to this story:

We can fool some of the creatures some of the time-

but you can't fool all of the creatures all of the time.

A Pest?

I peered at a rodent very tiny and
one would say CUTE
He climbed a tree, spoke to a squirrel
They partook of acorns
Then this Mouse was off to an RSVP
And needed to don a tailored suit
By nature, humans feared him —
He knew not why?
They always screamed in his presence
Always he scratched the top of his little
Head to figure out Why?
Can they be mistaken? Was he harmless indeed!
Even an elephant, as Gigantic, as it is,
Would always take heed!
It has been four score and two years ago since
One caring man,
Who made magic; Loved this rodent, believed in him,
Adopted him and made him come alive!
Now he is; along with his famous gal and pals,
A Booming, Billion Dollar Corporation!!

Do You Know Him? —
His side kick "Quacks" for a Living!

Cest La Vie-That's Life!

Hello my Love
How do you do?
Why could You not be True?
That's Life!

I thought, you felt
The same as I
But seems
I was a fool.
That's Life!

What did we have?
Or ought I ask Was it a
One-way street?
That's Life!

You loved me not
'Twas not your fault
I must admit defeat.
That's Life!

Love was my crutch
I had no clue
Therefore, we did
Not meet!
That's Life!

Is A Bird Free?

The birds I see up-in the tree
Are unlike the birds in the cage

The birds in the tree, so un-like
You and me, will never be seen in a rage

The birds in the tree are obviously Free!

They soar through the air with nary a care
And sing with the utmost glee

Oh, if only I were a bird!

I could wing, I could sing-Do most
Anything, you know, without saying a word

The birds in the cage are so, stifled within

They long for their home in the sky

They say not to you nor me

But you can see the woe in their eyes

One day, when life is fair
When man can finally care

Cages, we will no — longer find!

Peace at Last

Banished forever from Rodent Land, mice were termed," too tiny" to fit into the family of beavers, rats and shrews. Mice lacked the creativity of Beavers; mice lacked the Fierceness of Rats; And tiny little mice missed-out on the viciousness of their fellow brethren, the Shrews! Thus, their Banishment from Rodent Land! This message was gnawed and scratched on every tree-trunk, under every floating log and on the walls of every barn throughout Rodent Land. All of the Beavers, Rats, and Shrews put forth every effort to drive these tiny mice away. Oh, the beavers swatted the mice with their paddle-like tails; the rats roared at the mice with their meanest roars; and the shrews chewed at the heels of the mice with their razor sharp teeth! You should have seen the millions of tiny, mice scampering in all directions. What a woeful Sight!

I belong to the family of Doves and as I witnessed the fearful plight of the tiny creatures below, Instinct allowed me to relay this message to as many other birds flying by. This called for a retreat to our respective nests to help locate a new home for these tiny, harmless, creatures. Eventually, the other birds and I did just that! We came across a patch of land inhabited by a variety of small creatures, from all walks of, "creaturedom."

Now, named, "Mouseland" frogs were, once not allowed. It was not until the passing of the Amphibian Bill," which said, "All small creatures who inhabit both land and water, will now be accepted in Mouse land, especially frogs.

The first mice, which began to live in the land that is now named, Mouse land, had a very long and tough battle with the scorpions, lizards, and other small creatures, who were here first. Not only, were mice small, peace-loving creatures, they believed in the Golden Rule; "Do unto others as you would have them Do unto you." As a result, Mice vowed, the next land that they would call home would be solely for small, harmless, creatures such as themselves.

It just happened, that this patch of land, which was found for the mice, was so High not anyone could get over it, so Low not a soul could get under It. Thus, the story Goes; Our tiny, God-fearing, heroes found their Peace in the Valley, for the rest of the days of their Lives! Now, all God's children say, "Amen."

In Memoriam

The loss of a comrade brings woe to one's soul
To allow its consumption will sure take its toll
Cherish your memoirs, the good and the bad
Also the ones that were Happy and the ones that were sad
Your comrade would want you to forge on ahead
To follow your dreams and rise up from your bed
The soul of your comrade will soon be at peace
As quickly, you will realize
Your heart is free from grief.

Sprung!

Spring has sprung and
Oh to savor
The subtle signs of
Mother Nature
See the birds a-soaring High?
Or Hear them chirping as they nigh?
Do you peer at frogs a-hopping? Or
Catch a glimpse of children romping?
A duck a-quacking as it swims?
Then rest my case 'cause Spring is in!

The Signs

The rays of sun
The clouds above
The children's play
The vows of love
The leaves on trees
The flowers abloom
The threats of thunderstorms
That loom

The ocean waves, the surfers' boards
The beaches swarmed by bathers in hordes
Oh, how it makes me come alive
Despite the buzzing 'round the hives
These are the signs as you may know
When summertime replaces snow!

Limerick 1—Hillary

Up from New York, came a well-spoken
Democrat, named, Hillary.

She whole-heartedly saluted
The nations military!

Unbeknownst to her dismay
Her accounts, came up short
By the way.

It did not upset Hillary
Cause along came help;
Her auxiliary!

Limerick 2—Obama

*Our forty fourth president
Upon orating his final,
State of the union address;*

*Was sure that, it became, without a doubt
A success!*

*The republicans were meaner and,
claimed; it was leaner!*

*None-the-less, the address, crowned
Our 44th president; "His Eminence!"*

Molasses

Grasshoppers always hop about
That is how they earned their name
That is not half as we may presume
'Cause they instinctively chew on grasses

When these winged ones masticate,
The color is brown like molasses!

Grasshoppers are fun to catch
Because, they pose a challenge

Now, on that day, you do catch one
Be gentle; do not mishandle it!

You know why?
It may remind you of a famous cricket!

And make for a cute, green pet!

Milton Keynes UK
Ingram Content Group UK Ltd.
UKHW012144141023
430633UK00001B/77